IN THIS ISSUE:

I0393420

tour.sm TATTLER

ISSUE 04 APRIL 2017

PUBLISHER
Tourism Tattler (Pty) Ltd.
PO Box 891, Umhlanga Rocks, 4320
KwaZulu-Natal, South Africa.
Website: www.tourismtattler.com

EXECUTIVE EDITOR Des Langkilde
Cell: +27 (0)82 374 7260
Fax: +27 (0)86 651 8080
E-mail: editor@tourismtattler.com
Skype: tourismtattler

MAGAZINE ADVERTISING
ADVERTISING DIRECTOR Bev Langkilde
Cell: +27 (0)71 224 9971
Fax: +27 (0)86 656 3860
E-mail: bev@tourismtattler.com
Skype: bevtourismtattler

SUBSCRIPTIONS
http://eepurl.com/bocldD

BACK ISSUES (Click on the covers below).

▼ MAR 2017   ▼ FEB 2017   ▼ JAN 2017

▼ DEC 2016   ▼ NOV 2016   ▼ OCT 2016

▼ SEP 2016   ▼ AUG 2016   ▼ JUL 2016

▼ JUN 2016   ▼ MAY 2016   ▼ APR 2016

CONTENTS

EDITORIAL CONTRIBUTORS

Anna Pollock   Martin Janse van Vuuren
Annebeth Wijtenburg   Nawal du Toit
Guy Stehlik   Samantha Petersen
Jennifer Woodbridge   Tessa Buhrmann
Louis Nel

MAGAZINE SPONSORS

SUPPORTED CHARITIES

06 Diabetes South Africa   **28** National Sea Rescue Institute

ACCREDITATION

Official Travel Trade Journal and Media Partner to:

The Africa Travel Association (ATA)

Tel: +1 212 447 1357 • Email: info@africatravelassociation.org • Website: www.africatravelassociation.org

ATA is a division of the Corporate Council on Africa (CCA), and a registered non-profit trade association in the USA, with headquarters in Washington, DC and chapters around the world. ATA is dedicated to promoting travel and tourism to Africa and strengthening intra-Africa partnerships. Established in 1975, ATA provides services to both the public and private sectors of the industry.

The African Travel & Tourism Association (Atta)

Tel: +44 20 7937 4408 • Email: info@atta.travel • Website: www.atta.travel

Members in 22 African countries and 37 worldwide use Atta to: Network and collaborate with peers in African tourism; Grow their online presence with a branded profile; Ask and answer specialist questions and give advice; and Attend key industry events.

National Accommodation Association of South Africa (NAA-SA)

Tel: +27 86 186 2272 • Fax: +2786 225 9858 • Website: www.naa-sa.co.za

The NAA-SA is a network of mainly smaller accommodation providers around South Africa – from B&Bs in country towns offering comfortable personal service to luxurious boutique city lodges with those extra special touches – you're sure to find a suitable place, and at the same time feel confident that your stay at an NAA-SA member's establishment will meet your requirements.

Regional Tourism Organisation of Southern Africa (RETOSA)

Tel: +27 11 315 2420/1 • Fax: +27 11 315 2422 • Website: www.retosa.co.za

RETOSA is a Southern African Development Community (SADC) institution responsible for tourism growth and development. RETOSA's aims are to increase tourist arrivals to the region through. RETOSA Member States are Angola, Botswana, DR Congo, Lesotho, Madagascar, Malawi, Mauritius, Mozambique, Namibia, Seychelles, South Africa, Swaziland, Tanzania, Zambia and Zimbabwe.

Southern African Vehicle Rental and Leasing Association (SAVRALA)

Contact: manager@savrala.co.za • Website: www.savrala.co.za

Founded in the 1970's, SAVRALA is the representative voice of Southern Africa's vehicle rental, leasing and fleet management sector. Our members have a combined national footprint with more than 600 branches countrywide. SAVRALA are instrumental in steering industry standards and continuously strive to protect both their members' interests, and those of the public, and are therefore widely respected within corporate and government sectors.

Seychelles Hospitality & Tourism Association (SHTA)

Tel: +248 432 5560 • Fax: +248 422 5718 • Website: www.shta.sc

The Seychelles Hospitality and Tourism Association was created in 2002 when the Seychelles Hotel Association merged with the Seychelles Hotel and Guesthouse Association. SHTA's primary focus is to unite all Seychelles tourism industry stakeholders under one association in order to be better prepared to defend the interest of the industry and its sustainability as the pillar of the country's economy.

International Coalition of Tourism Partners (ICTP)

Website: www.tourismpartners.org

ICTP is a travel and tourism coalition of global destinations committed to Quality Services and Green Growth.

International Institute for Peace through Tourism

Website: www.iipt.org

IIPT is dedicated to fostering tourism initiatives that contribute to international understanding and cooperation.

ITB Asia 2017

Website: www.itb-asia.com

25 to 27 October 2017 Marina Bay Sands®, Singapore.

ITB Asia is the leading B2B travel trade event for the entire Asia-Pacific region.

Tourism, Hotel Investment and Networking Conference 2017

Website: www.thincafrica..com

THINC Africa 2017 takes place in Cape Town, South Africa from 6-7 September.

The Hotel Show Africa 2017

Website: TheHotelShowAfrica.com

Thousands of hospitality professionals from around the world will be at Gallagher Convention Centre in Johannesburg from 25-27 June.

The Safari Awards

Website: www.safariawards.com

Safari Award finalists are amongst the top 3% in Africa and the winners are unquestionably the best.

PAHTC 2017

Website: www.panafricanhealthtourismcongress.com

08-09 June 2017 at the City of uMhlathuze in KwaZulu-Natal, South Africa.

The Pan-African Health Tourism Congress is being staged to address the interests and needs of Health Tourism Stakeholders in Africa.

08-09 June 2017

Register Today

+27 11 040 7352
registrar@mcgroup.co.za

PAN-AFRICAN
HEALTH TOURISM
CONGRESS

BUSINESS OPPORTUNITY FAIR & EXHIBITION

uMfolozi Hotel Casino & Convention Centre | uMhlathuze, KwaZulu-Natal, South Africa

www.panafricanhealthtourismcongress.com

HOST CITY

SUPPORTING PARTNERS

ASSOCIATE PARTNER

MEDIA PARTNER

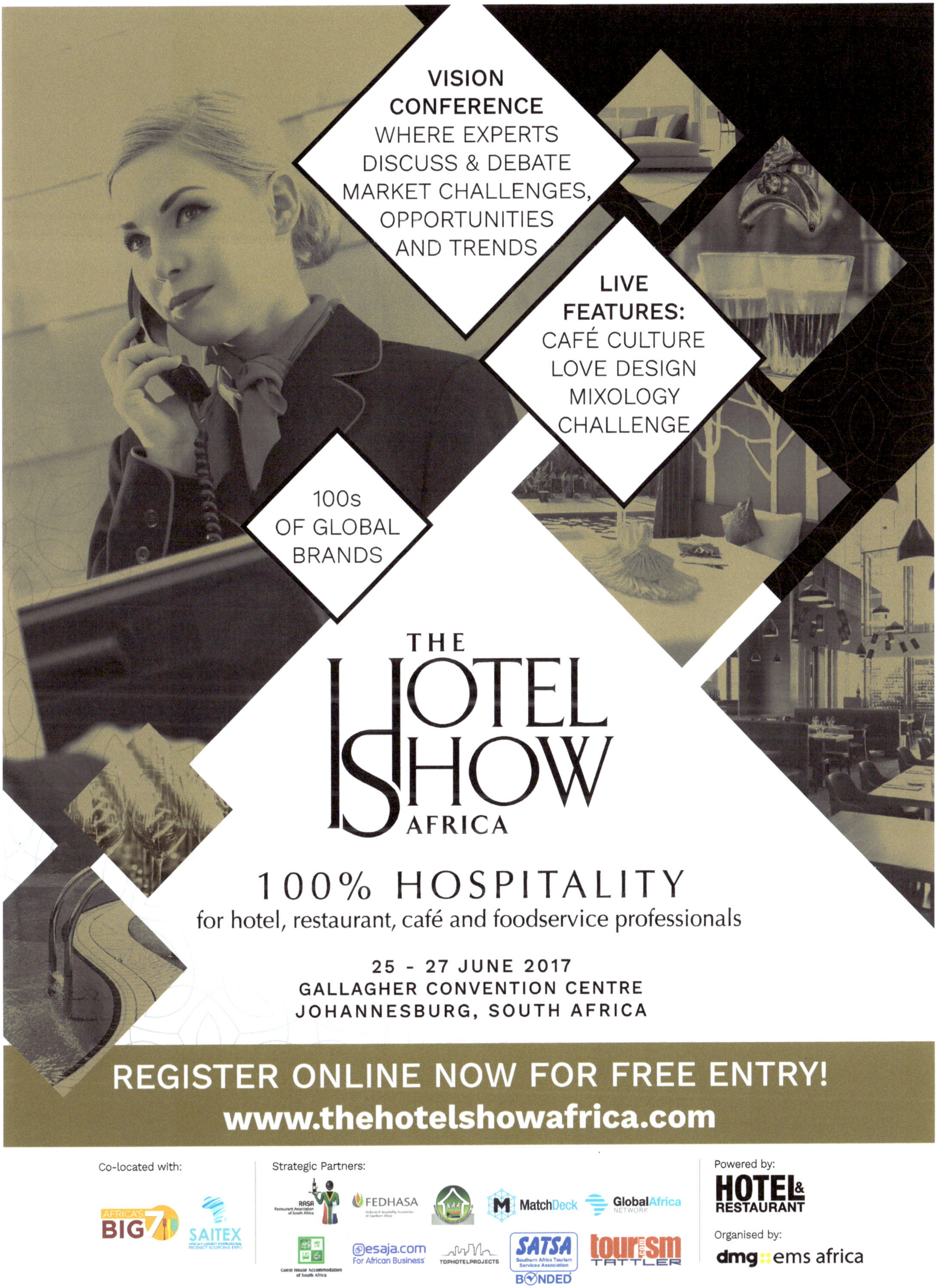

VISION CONFERENCE
WHERE EXPERTS DISCUSS & DEBATE MARKET CHALLENGES, OPPORTUNITIES AND TRENDS

LIVE FEATURES:
CAFÉ CULTURE
LOVE DESIGN
MIXOLOGY CHALLENGE

100s OF GLOBAL BRANDS

THE Hotel Show AFRICA

100% HOSPITALITY
for hotel, restaurant, café and foodservice professionals

25 - 27 JUNE 2017
GALLAGHER CONVENTION CENTRE
JOHANNESBURG, SOUTH AFRICA

REGISTER ONLINE NOW FOR FREE ENTRY!
www.thehotelshowafrica.com

Co-located with:

Strategic Partners:

Powered by:

Organised by:

Common Symptoms of
DIABETES

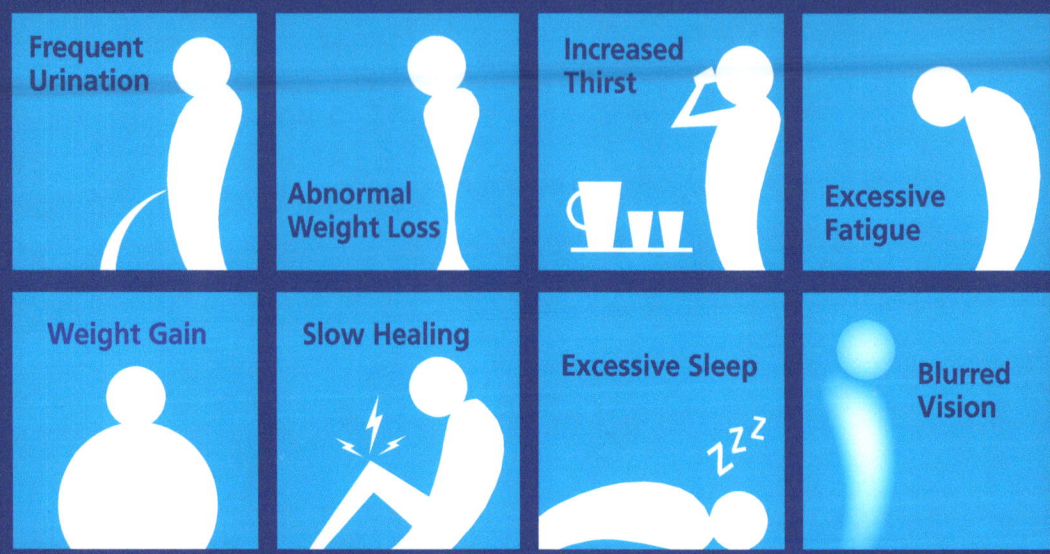

Frequent Urination

Abnormal Weight Loss

Increased Thirst

Excessive Fatigue

Weight Gain

Slow Healing

Excessive Sleep

Blurred Vision

If you experience any of these symptoms, you may be diabetic.

422 MILLION
adults have diabetes
That's 1 person in 11

Prevention is better than cure.
Don't wait until it's too late. Get self-care advice today.

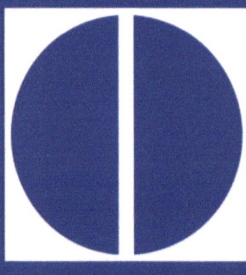

Diabetes South Africa

Tel: +27 (0)21 425 4440
national@diabetessa.org.za

Facebook.com/Diabetes.South.Africa
www.diabetessa.org.za

ARMENIA	BRAZIL	COLOMBIA	GEORGIA	KOREA	SEYCHELLES	ZIMBABWE
Vahan Martirosyan	Márcio Favilla	Jaime Sanclemente	Zurab Pololikashvili	Young-shim Dho	Alain St. Ange	Walter Mzembi

THE RACE FOR UNWTO SECRETARY-GENERAL

The United Nations World Tourism Organisation (UNWTO) has announced the names of the seven candidates who will be competing in the race for the top tourism industry post of Secretary-General to replace Taleb Rifai when his term ends in December this year.

By **Des Langkilde**.

The governments of UNWTO member states Armenia, Brazil, Colombia, Georgia, Korea, Seychelles and Zimbabwe have endorsed their respective candidates for election to the post, which is due to take place during the UNWTO Executive Council meeting scheduled to be held in Madrid, Spain on 11 May 2017.

After 42 years of European, North American, and Asian leadership domination, Africa finally has a chance to take the helm and steer the UNWTO into the global future of tourism as the race for the top post heats up. France, Austria, Mexico, and Jordan have led the UNWTO thus far, with France and Jordan having served two four-year terms.

Since the UNWTO started operations in November 1974 as the United Nations agency responsible for the promotion of responsible, sustainable and universally accessible tourism, it has not had an African country Secretary-General at the helm. This despite the fact that one the original aims of the International Congress of Official Tourist Traffic Associations (ICOTT) – the precursor to UNWTO founded in 1920 – was, and still is, to "extract the best out of tourism as an international trade component and as an economic development strategy for developing nations."

As the highest office in the global tourism industry, the candidate who wins the race for the post of Secretary-General will influence not only his or her own continent and country's future, but the future of global issues such air access and the development of sustainable tourism for the next four years (2018-2021), which is why it is so important to have a non-partisan country leader with proven experience, ethics, and vision to win this election.

As a media publisher of travel trade news and editorial content, I've researched the backgrounds and followed the campaign speeches of most of the candidates, and I can honestly say that the Seychelles candidate, Alain St.Ange stands out most prominently from the crowd.

Perhaps I'm being biased as St.Ange is the only candidate whom I have personally met. He is also the only candidate who keeps the media informed on his campaign progress, who actually replies to emails and who engages regularly on social media. In fact, when St.Ange still held the position of Seychelles Minister responsible for Tourism, Civil Aviation, Ports and Marine, he was the only Minister I know of who personally made the effort to meet and greet hosted media late at night on arrival at the islands Mahé airport.

Background

St.Ange has been working in the tourism industry since 2009. He studied Hotel Management and Tourism at schools in Germany and France before launching his own career in hospitality. He held several positions with hotels and restaurants in Seychelles, the Channel Islands, and Australia before landing the role of General Manager for Denis Island, a private resort in Seychelles. It was this extensive experience in the hospitality field, in addition to his political upbringing, that eventually led him to be appointed as the Director of Marketing for Seychelles. After one year of service, he was promoted to the position of CEO of the Seychelles Tourism Board. In 2012 he was instrumental in founding the Indian Ocean Vanilla Islands Regional Organisation – a consortium designed to combine the strengths of the islands located in the Indian Ocean to present a strong front in a competitive market – to which St.Ange was appointed as the first president. In a 2012 cabinet reshuffle he was appointed as Minister of Tourism and Culture, and subsequently as the Seychelles Minister responsible for Tourism, Civil Aviation, Ports and Marine. He resigned from his Ministerial post in January 2017 to pursue the UNWTO Secretary-General position. Among his many accomplishments, St.Ange initiated the Carnaval International de Victoria in 2011 – an annual event that not only celebrates culture and diversity but has had a significant impact on Seychelles tourism arrival figures and gained the country countless friends in the media and significant international exposure. St.Ange is fluent in English, French and Creole, and speaks German, which makes him qualified to represent various walks of society.

While all seven candidates have their own distinguished backgrounds and have accumulated the requisite experience, what is more important, is what they plan to do if elected as the next Secretary-General.

St.Ange understands that it is not a country's government that builds a tourism industry – its people do. Those entrepreneurs who invest in creating the products, in employing and training their staff to provide excellent service, the efforts of a myriad of allied service providers, and above all, the citizens themselves who combine to provide memorable experiences and fond memories as hosts to their international guests – they build the tourism industry.

On the subject of Safety & Security, one of the notable changes to the UNWTO's current structure that Alain mentions in his Seven-Point-Plan Statement of Intent, is to establish Regional Offices in Member States with a 'field presence' person to "…ensure that partner organisations and the media join together to plan the most suitable course of action for the Member States." He also points out that "The UNWTO must appreciate the importance of the media in this challenge, and it is only by engaging with them as partners that they will be able to appreciate the destructive potential of insecurity on the tourism industry."

But seeing as my vote, or yours for that matter doesn't count (unless you serve on the UNWTO Executive Council of course), let's hope that common sense rather than political manoeuvring prevails in the upcoming elections on 11 May.

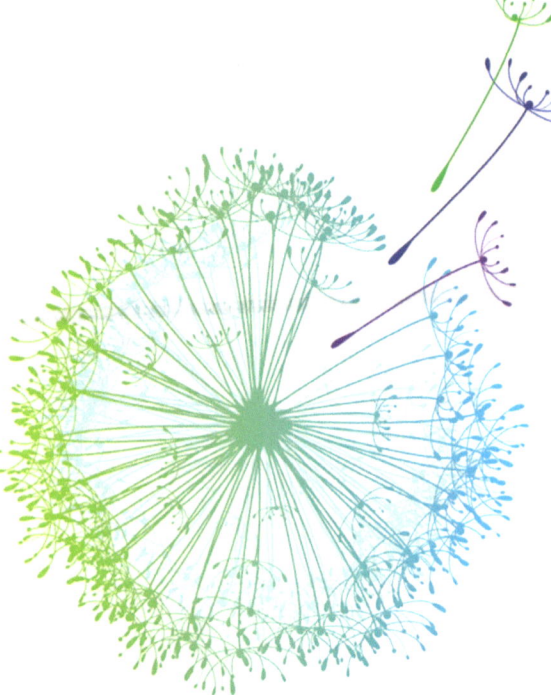

> 66 *Every year, 1.2 billion people travel abroad. These, and the billions more who travel domestically, create a sector which contributes 10% of global GDP to the world's economies and 1 in 11 jobs. Tourism has become a passport to prosperity, a driver of peace, and a transformative force for improving millions of lives.* 99
> **Taleb Rifai - UNWTO Secretary General.**

SUPPORTING THE 2017 INTERNATIONAL YEAR OF SUSTAINABLE TOURISM FOR DEVELOPMENT

As an international influence for travel in the content of Africa, Tourism Tattler has joined global media in promoting the aims and aspirations of the International Year of Sustainable Tourism for Development 2017. Through a series of editorial features published throughout this year, Tourism Tattler is profiling African destinations and Africa based tourism products and services who meet and in many cases exceed, sustainable tourism practices in their business operations.

Officially launched at the FITUR International Tourism Fair in Madrid, Spain, on 18 January 2017, the UNWTO International Year of Sustainable Tourism for Development 2017 aims to establish twelve months of global action aimed at advancing sustainable tourism contribution towards the United Nations 2030 Agenda for Sustainable Development.

Speaking at the launch, United Nations Secretary-General, Antonio Guterres, said: "The world can and must harness the power of tourism as we strive to carry out the 2030 Agenda for Sustainable Development. Three of the 17 Sustainable Development Goals (SDGs) include targets that relate to tourism: Goal 8 on promoting growth and decent work, Goal 12 on ensuring sustainable consumption and production, and Goal 14 on conserving marine resources. But tourism also cuts across so many different areas of life and involves so many different economic sectors and socio-cultural currents, that it is connected to the entire Agenda. Beyond the measurable advances that tourism can make possible, it is also a bridge to better mutual understanding among people from all walks of life."

Sustainable Tourism Consumption

The UNWTO has been appointed to lead the 10-Year Framework of Programmes on Sustainable Consumption and Production Patterns (10YFP) Sustainable Tourism Programme (STP) - a collaborative platform to bring together existing initiatives and partnerships and facilitate new projects and activities to accelerate the shift to sustainable consumption and production (SCP) in tourism.

As an implementation mechanism, the vision of the 10YFP STP is for a tourism sector that has globally adopted SCP resulting in enhanced environmental and social outcomes and improved economic performance. *Read more at* www.sdt.unwto.org.

Sustainable Tourism and Climate Change

According to Wikipedia, sustainable tourism is the concept of visiting a place as a tourist and trying to make only a positive impact on the environment, society and economy. Given that without travel there is no tourism, the article cites aviation as being the greatest contributor to tourism's effect on climate change, claiming that 72% of tourism's CO_2 emissions come from transportation, 24% from accommodations, and 4% from local activities.

Sustainable Tourism Guidelines

The Global Sustainable Tourism Council has developed criteria and suggested indicators for Hotels, which aim to provide a common understanding of sustainable tourism and provide a benchmark for the minimum standards that a hotel should aspire to reach. *Download the GSTC Hotel Criteria at* www.gstcouncil.org.

Some of the uses of the criteria include:
- A basis for sustainability certification.
- Guidelines for businesses to become more sustainable, and for businesses to choose sustainable tourism programmes that fulfil these global criteria.
- Provide market access.
- For consumers to identify sound sustainable tourism businesses.
- For media to recognise sustainable tourism providers.
- Help certification bodies to ensure that their standards meet a broadly-accepted baseline.
- Offer governmental, non-governmental, and private sector programmes a starting point for developing sustainable tourism requirements.
- Provide guidelines to education and training bodies.
- Demonstrate leadership that inspires others to act.

The Criteria indicate what *should* be done, not *how* to do it or whether the goal has been achieved. This role is fulfilled by performance indicators, associated educational materials, and access to tools for implementation, all of which are an indispensable complement to the GSTC Criteria.

HOME SEARCH ⊙ ABOUT ⊙ GET INVOLVED ⊙ BLOG ⊙ CONTACT US | GET LISTED ON ECO ATLAS ✓

Launching Africa's sustainable tourism gems this month with a selection of South Africa's eco-friendly hotels and lodges, Tourism Tattler has partnered with Eco Atlas – an award winning eco-travel choice website. Where a featured eco-friendly property is already listed on Eco Atlas, we've shown the applicable icons.

RESOURCE USE

Water Saving: 3 or more of the following practices in place: a no-leak policy, water audit, flow restrictors on taps and shower heads, dual flush toilet cisterns, harvesting rain water, utilising waste water (grey water), only watering early morning and evening, alien tree removal, planting water wise, drip irrigation system, compost toilet, garden well mulched.

Energy Saving: 3 or more of the following practices in place: energy A- rated appliances, low energy bulbs, geezer blankets and/or timers, established electricity strategy such as switching off appliances and lights when not being used.

Recycling: Established policy to reduce and re-use waste, the recycling of any of the following resources: Paper, Glass, Tin, Plastic and Organic Matter, on-site composting and wormeries.

Renewable Energy: Utilising solar and/or wind energy through solar panels and/or wind turbines.

Green Design: Incorporated into the design of the building: proper insulation, sustainable and renewable building materials, maximising light and energy from the sun, building with recycled materials, non-toxic paints and other building materials, water and energy efficiency.

Carbon Neutral: Planting of trees to off-set the carbon footprint of the establishment and its guests.

EARTH FRIENDLY

Eco Cleaning Agents: utilising or selling products that are fully biodegradable, free of harmful chemicals and not tested on animals.

Eco Body Products: Utilising or selling body products that are fully biodegradable, free of harmful chemicals and not tested on animals.

Eco Packaging: Utilising or selling fully biodegradable packaging and take-away containers made from renewable resources. Accepting returns on product packaging for re-use.

PEOPLE AND EARTH

Biodiversity: no use of pesticides or poisons, planting only indigenous, conservation of indigenous flora and fauna on your property, alien vegetation removal and rehabilitation of indigenous.

Local Products: utilising products grown or manufactured within a 100km radius, the producing or selling of local products.

Organic Food: Utilising or selling food that is produced using a system that sustains the health of soils, ecosystems and people without the use of inputs with adverse effects for biodiversity.

Fair Trade: selling products or implementing policies which contribute to sustainable development by offering better trading conditions to, and securing the rights of, marginalized producers and workers. Registered with Fair Trade Tourism or Fair Trade Label SA.

Empowerment: Skills development, training and profit share programmes which empower staff and enable better working conditions and work opportunities.

ANIMAL FRIENDLY

Free Range Chicken: raised in a humane manner with freedom to roam and constant access to vegetation , fresh air and fresh water. Chickens free of hormones and antibiotics (check with your supplier if they meet all these requirements)

Free Range Eggs: chickens raised in a humane manner with freedom to roam and constant access to vegetation, fresh air and fresh water. Chickens free of hormones and antibiotics (check with your supplier if they meet all these requirements)

Badger Friendly Honey: utilising or selling honey accredited with the Endangered Wildlife Trust certificate to ensure no honey badgers are harmed in the production of the honey.

Ethically Farmed Products: utilising or selling free range meat and/or wool products that are have wildlife friendly management strategies which do not include the trapping, hunting, poisoning and killing of predators. Fair Game endorsed products.

Sustainable Fishing: utilising, promoting or selling sustainable seafood from well managed fisheries as listed in the South African Sustainable Seafood Initiative (SASSI).

Free Range Pork: Raised in a humane manner with freedom to roam outdoors and constant access to vegetation, fresh air and fresh water. Pigs free of hormones and antibiotics and their feed free of animal by-products (check with your supplier if they meet all these requirements)

Veg Or Vegan: Serving purely vegetarian or vegan food, thereby providing healthy eating alternatives and decreasing the amount of natural resources used in the production of food.

2017
INTERNATIONAL YEAR
OF SUSTAINABLE TOURISM
FOR DEVELOPMENT

UNWTO

SUSTAINABLE TOURISM
Interview with Lalibela Private Game Reserve

With 2017 being the UNWTO International Year of Sustainable Tourism for Development, I wanted to find out how a Big-5 safari attraction implements sustainable tourism practices and markets these attributes to guests and suppliers.

By **Des Langkilde**.

According to UNWTO, the 2017 theme provides *'a unique opportunity to raise awareness on the contribution of sustainable tourism to development among public and private sector decision-makers and the public, while mobilising all stakeholders to work together in making tourism a catalyst for positive change'*.

With this in mind, I interviewed Vernon Wait, Marketing Director at Lalibela Private Game Reserve in the Eastern Cape Province of South Africa to find answers. *Note: TT is Tourism Tattler and VW is Vernon Wait.*

TT: Why is sustainable tourism an important component in developing a game reserve?

VW: As custodians of large tracts of a country's natural resources and cultural heritage, private landowners who operate as commercial enterprises and cater to the needs of tourists have a duty of care - not only to the safety of their guests but also to protect the environment, to manage the resources effectively, to enhance the lives of surrounding communities, and to minimise the impact of their activities on the environment.

TT: How does Lalibela communicate sustainable tourism to guests?

VW: Seeing as sustainability covers so many aspects, it really is a balancing act. For example, one of our initiatives aimed at enhancing the environment and minimising climate change concerns is to rehabilitate the land by eradicating alien invasive trees, which not only use a lot of scarce water but also change the soil structure and silt up river courses.

Obviously, this is a long term project and it does create some unsightly activity. So when guests arrive at Lalibela, we have a short orientation programme where we show a video clip to educate them on the need for, and long-term benefits of, this initiative. In addition, our rangers explain the reasons for this programme during game drives.

*Read more about the **Enviro Rehab Project** here, or watch the **video** here.*

TT: What's your biggest challenge in communicating sustainability?

VW: Well, as I said in answer to your first question, sustainability covers a lot of aspects, many of which happen behind the scenes and are difficult to communicate. But let's look at each of these in turn.

Firstly, on the safety of guests aspect our public liability insurance complies with the European Community Directive relating to the Package Holidays and Travel Trade Act and includes medical evacuation cover for guests in the unlikely event of an accident while on the reserve. We also ensure that our suppliers have appropriate insurance in place and that they, in turn, ensure that their international clients have travel insurance in place.

Then, on the environment and resource management aspect, we've already discussed the land rehabilitation initiative but in addition to this we commissioned a team of game management experts to determine the ideal carrying capacity of game on the reserve, based on the five flora biomes found here and purchased significant numbers of plains game to balance the number of predators that Lalibela has. In fact, Lalibela has the densest population of free-roaming predators in the Eastern Cape.

*Read more about the **Game Capacity at Big-5 Reserves** here, and about **Game Repopulation** here.*

Aerial view of Tree Tops Safari Lodge at Lalibela Private Game Reserve.

TT: **How do you engage the local community in what you do?**

VW: Lalibela plays a vital role in the upliftment of communities surrounding the reserve, especially women. Traditionally, rural women were restricted to menial employment opportunities, which often meant that they migrated to the cities, which in turn lead to breaking up families as children were left behind with grandparents. Being one of the largest employers between Port Elizabeth and Grahamstown, and being able to offer career opportunities for women, means that Lalibela has played a significant role in the upliftment of rural women since it first opened in 2002.

Since the sale of Lalibela to new owners, we have purchased significant additional land, and we are in the process of establishing a new 5 room (10-bed) lodge as well as adding 2 rooms (4 beds), which will create still more opportunities for both men and women in the surrounding rural communities. We have a firm policy in place whereby we employ people from the community and will only employ from outside the community if the skills set is not available. Constant training and upliftment also play a role in ensuring a better local skills base.

*Read more about the **sale of Lalibela** here.*

TT: **How do you engage your suppliers in what you do?**

VW: Itineraries to Africa can be complicated and require specialised knowledge, so as a safari property Lalibela thinks long term, and we build up strong relationships with suppliers in the belief that we are there to support each other in our respective sustainable tourism goals. Looking forward into this year, we are planning to become a signatory in support of the UNWTO Private Sector Commitment to the UNWTO Global Code of Ethics for Tourism. I think that the ethics of social responsibility that are contained in the Code are principles that we should all aspire to uphold.

*Download the **UNWTO Global Code of Ethics for Tourism** PDF here.*

TT: **What is unique or innovative about your marketing and communication approach?**

VW: We are strong believers in knowledge sharing for the greater good of the tourism industry as a whole. For example just look at the number of articles that we've sponsored in your own publication. In addition, our experienced and knowledgeable field guides educate guests on conservation and environmental issues. When guests arrive, they are assigned a guide. The guide not only takes them on game drives but also joins them at evening meals, either in the lodge restaurant or around the open-air boma, to engage in conversation and to answer questions.

We also offer child-friendly safaris at one of our lodges. The children's game drive has been specially designed for young children, with their own game ranger, Children's Programme Coordinator, and game-viewing vehicle. There is also a children's play centre and the accommodation caters to families, as do the meal arrangements.

*Read more about **WiFi at Safari Lodges** here, about **Making the Most of a Safari in the Rain** here, and about **Child-Friendly Safaris** here.*

TT: **What have you learned about marketing sustainable tourism so far, what works and what doesn't?**

VW: One thing we don't do, and I caution anyone in the travel trade reading this not to even try, is engage in greenwashing If you're going to commit to sustainable tourism practices, don't just create the perception that your products, aims or policies are environmentally friendly – walk the talk – demonstrate your commitment through tangible initiatives and actions, and communicate these outcomes to your communities, to your staff, to your guests, and to your suppliers. Get them involved. Sustainable tourism is not a stand-alone philosophy, it's a collective aspiration that can only work for the good of people and the planet if we work as one. **t**

ECO-FRIENDLY
HOTELS & LODGES

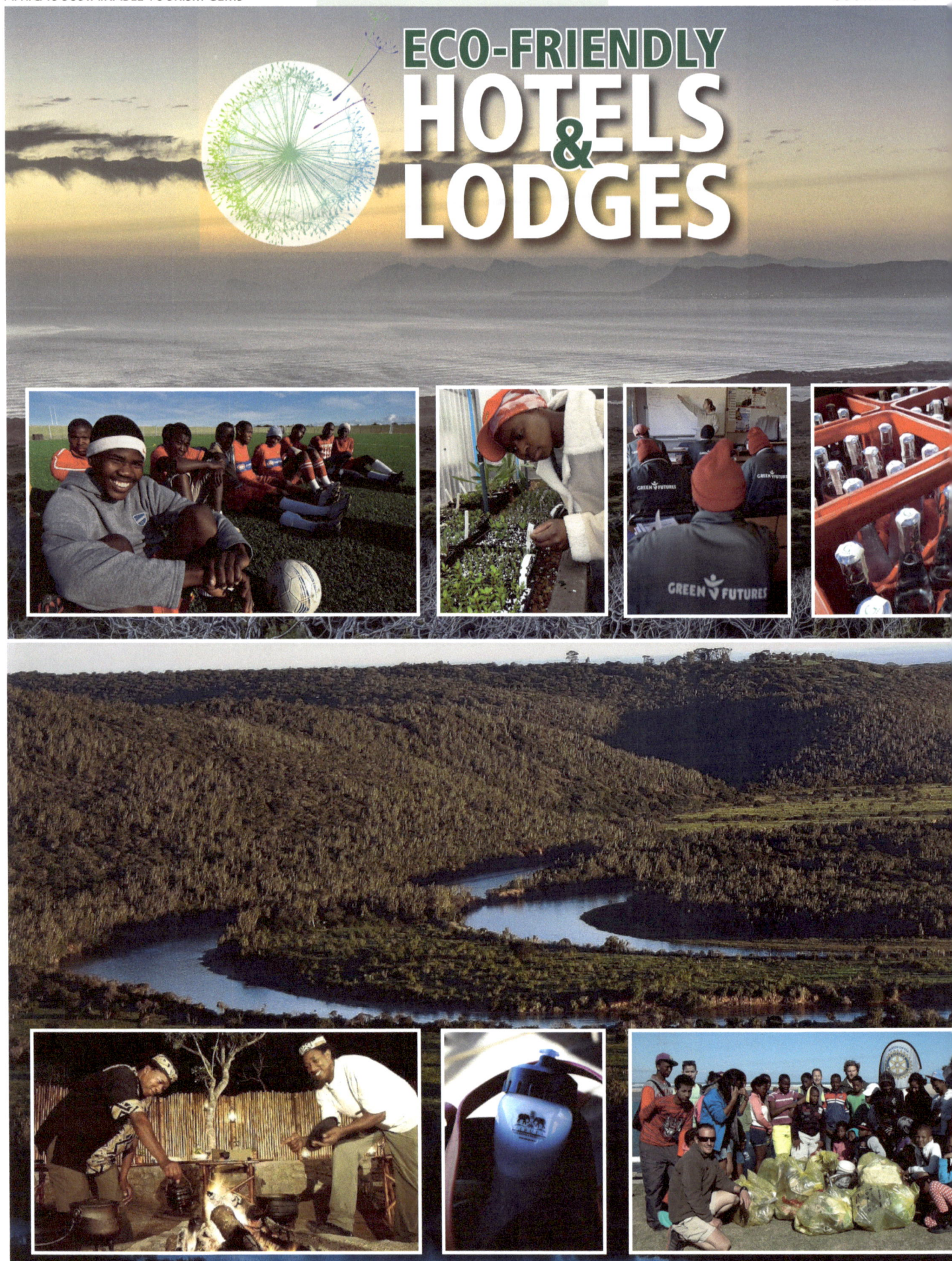

Grootbos Forest Lodge

Nestled in ancient Milkweed forests on the slope of a 2500 hectare botanical treasure trove between mountain and sea, Forest Lodge is strategically placed to provide guests with privacy and uninterrupted panoramic views over Walker Bay to De Kelders and Gansbaai along the scenic Cape Whale Coast route.

Grootbos Private Nature Reserve has an enviable track history of implementing sustainable tourism initiatives. So successful in fact, that a separate NPO was formed to help other hospitality businesses implement their own 'green' initiatives.

The Grootbos Foundation facilitates three integrated programmes: 'Green Futures' which focuses on conservation, the 'Football Foundation' which focuses on utilising sport for development, and 'Siyakhula' which focuses on the creation of sustainable livelihoods.

For more about Grootbos's sustainable tourism development, read our review 'How to Apply Responsible Tourism Practices' or 'Ecotourism: A Case Study' and our Property Review on the reserve and the three lodges; Forest Lodge, Garden Lodge and the Villa. But why take our word for it – experience Grootbos yourself.

QUICK LINKS:

✉ bookings@grootbos.co.za

🏠 www.grootbos.com

▶ GrootbosReserve

📞 +27 (0) 28 384 8008

f 🐦 @Grootbos

PACK for a PURPOSE

eco ATLAS RATING

Sibuya Game Reserve and Tented Camps

Located on the coast at Kenton on Sea in the Eastern Cape and spanning the magnificent Kariega Estuary on its course to meet the warm Indian Ocean, the malaria-free Sibuya Game Reserve is South Africa's only game reserve accessed solely by boat.

Sibuya provides a personalised African bush experience that is acknowledged as being ecologically, socially and financially sustainable.

A few of the myriad ways that Subuya maintains its low-impact, sustainable tourism reputation as a Big-5 safari attraction include: recruiting and training staff from the local community; purchasing goods and services locally, on-site recycling and composting; restricting energy consumption to solar power, using low-energy light bulbs and slow-burning lanterns; using CFC-free refrigeration and gas grillers and hobs for cooking; providing guests with still-water decanters and re-usable water bottles (Sibuya recently installed a desalination plant to produce their own prepared water for decanters and ice) – the list is extensive and includes ongoing environmental rehabilitation of purchased farmland surrounding the reserve.

Browse through the links below or better yet, make a booking.

QUICK LINKS:

✉ reservations@sibuya.co.za

🏠 www.sibuya.co.za

📞 +27 (0)46 648 1040

ⓞ f 🐦 @SibuyaGameRes

📍 Listed on Africa Adventure Travel GeoDirectory HERE.

eco ATLAS RATING    ▶

Safari Lodge at Amakhala Game Reserve

African tribal design-inspired owners and artists, Mike and Justine Weeks' meticulous attention to detail is reflected in the fine African beadwork and handcrafted designs that are evident throughout the prestigious Safari Lodge on the northern boundary of Amakhala Game Reserve.

But Amakhala Safari Lodge is more than just a celebration of tribal culture. Through the Amakhala Foundation, founded in 2009 and funded through guest bed levies and donations, Safari Lodge contributes significantly to local community education, training, HIV/AIDS awareness and support, and income generation through the Amakhala Craft Centre.

In addition, the Conservation Centre established in 2013, provides support for research and monitoring, environmental education and conservation initiatives. *Read more about the work of the Amakhala Foundation HERE*.

Amakhala Safari Lodge's responsible tourism and Ecotourism initiatives focus on six guiding principles, namely (1) Minimising environmental impact, (2) Building cultural awareness and respect, (3) Providing positive experiences for both visitors and hosts, (4) Ensuring direct financial benefits for conservation and (5) for local people, and (6) Raising sensitivity to South Africa's political, environmental and social climate. *Read more HERE*.

QUICK LINKS:

📞 +27 (0)82 659 1796   f @amakhalareserve

✉ safari@amakhala.co.za   🐦 @amakhala

🏠 www.amakhala.co.za   ▶ Amakhala Volunteers

Tswalu Kalahari Private Game Reserve

As South Africa's largest private game reserve Tswalu exists primarily as a conservation project started 20 years ago, which seeks to restore denuded farmlands in the Northern Cape's Kalahari savannah eco-system.

Today Tswalu covers an area of over 1,000 sqm and is an ecological work in progress, contributing significantly to biodiversity conservation and recognised as a renowned centre of research. The Tswalu Foundation was established to provide support to a range of scientific research projects, including projects to understand the impact that climate change will have on marginal species such as the endangered pangolin.

The reserve offers an authentic African wildlife experience with a limited number of beds (30 in total) and just seven safari vehicles traversing the area at any one time. While Tswalu is home to most of the "charismatic" African big game species, the arid habitat also supports an array of smaller animals, birds and plants and guests are encouraged to explore all aspects of the eco system.

The word 'Tswalu' means *'a new beginning'* and Tswalu Kalahari is driven by two ambitions: to create an inspirational experience for its guests; and a conservation vision, to restore the Kalahari to itself. These two goals sit in perfect equilibrium with each guest contributing directly to the sustainability of the reserve in a true model of eco-tourism.

QUICK LINKS:

✉ res@tswalu.com   🏠 www.tswalu.com   📞 +27 (0)53 781 9331

 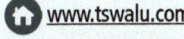 

@TswaluKalahari / @Tswalu

UNSUSTAINABLE AVIATION?

According to the Partnership for Open and Fair Skies, Gulf-owned Qatar Airways, Etihad Airways and Emirates aim to dominate global aviation by exploiting Open Skies policy and using subsidies to exploit their unfettered access to the US market, thereby threatening the US airline industry, airline jobs and the US economy.

The US Open Skies Debate

However, an industry analysis released by the Business Travel Coalition claims that the Partnership for Open and Fair Skies anti-Gulf airline campaign is "Spinning to the core of the abyss." Here's the full release:

The abyss of spin is when someone is so desperate to concoct a compelling story that they become confused about whether they are on False Facts 1.0 or 2.0 or 3.0. Anti-Open Skies advocates and their political campaign to stamp out airline competition has reached this lowly distinction. As a result, their attempt to resuscitate their failed advocacy campaign increasingly looks like a Three Stooges episode.

The Partnership for Open and Fair Skies ("Partnership"), more aptly, the Partnership for Less Consumer Choice and Higher Airfares, just released a newspaper ad claiming a single Emirates Airline Newark-Athens-Dubai flight -- there has been no U.S.-Greece year-round non-stop air service for five years because U.S. airlines have chosen not to offer it -- puts 10 million American jobs at risk.

The same group, led by Delta Air Lines, then released a cable television commercial claiming competition with Emirates Airline, Etihad Airways and Qatar Airways ("Gulf Carriers") puts 1.2 million U.S. airline jobs at risk, even though the U.S. Department of Transportation's ("DOT") Bureau of Transportation Statistics indicates that as of January 2017 there are only 687,000 full and part-time U.S. airline employees. To add to the confusion, the Association of Flight Attendants, a member of the Partnership, recently testified before the U.S. Congress that 300,000 U.S. airline jobs are at risk.

So which number is accurate? Of course, the answer is none of them. They are political talking points with no basis in reality. The largest U.S. airlines are making record-setting profits because there is too little, not too much, competition.

U.S. airline jobs have soared by over 15 percent in the past two years. In 2016 alone employee profit sharing payouts at Delta Air Lines totalled $1.1 billion (down from $1.5 billion in 2015, the largest payout in the history of corporate profit sharing programs), $628 million at United Airlines and $314 million at American Airlines.

Facts are stubborn things. The reality is that the Partnership cannot point to a single Delta Air Lines, American Airlines or United Airlines ("Big 3") widebody aircraft that has been parked or a single employee that has been furloughed due to competition with Gulf Carriers. Their entire narrative is fiction. All their widebody aircraft and the crew for them are flying and helping the Big 3 continue to rake in record profits.

One cannot blame the Partnership for tripping over their False Facts. They have so many that they cannot help but step on one at every turn. In 2015 and 2016, the Partnership claimed each widebody flight not operated due to Gulf Carrier competition cost 800 jobs. That same claim in 2017 by the Partnership morphed into 1,500 jobs. In a recent written statement to the U.S. Congress, the Air Line Pilots Association ("ALPA"), also a member of the Partnership, used the old False Fact 1.0 that 800 jobs are lost. Apparently, ALPA didn't get the memo from the Partnership that False Fact 1.0 had failed so they were upgrading to False Fact 2.0. However, ALPA should not feel singled out. Americans for Fair Skies, another advocacy group for the anti-Open Skies U.S. airlines, apparently did not receive that memo either. That group's website still displays False Fact 1.0.

Many industry observers wonder why the Big 3 failed to take the customary and longstanding course of filing an International Air Transportation Fair Competitive Practices Act ("IATFCPA") complaint with DOT. That is the time-honored action U.S. airlines have taken when they have a grievance with foreign airline competitors.

The explanation is simple: IATFCPA is a fact-based review and the Big 3 know they cannot make a case under IATFCPA's exacting factual requirements. The Big 3 and the Partnership assert their case is "irrefutable." However, their failure to file an IATFCPA complaint is most telling. They know False Facts 1.0, 2.0 and beyond simply won't cut it in a DOT review. But, disingenuously, they are hoping these False Facts nonetheless are sufficient for their political campaign.

About the Partnership for Open & Fair Skies: *This partnership is a coalition composed of American Airlines, Delta Air Lines and United Airlines, along with the Air Line Pilots Association, Int'l, the Allied Pilots Association, the Airline Division of the International Brotherhood of Teamsters, the Association of Flight Attendants-CWA, the Association of Professional Flight Attendants, the Communications Workers of America and the Southwest Airlines Pilots' Association.* www.openandfairskies.com

About the Business Travel Coalition: *Founded in 1994, the mission of Business Travel Coalition is to interpret industry and government policies and practices and provide a platform so that the managed travel community can influence issues of strategic importance to their organisations.* www.businesstravelcoalition.com

About OpenSkies.travel: *The mission of OpenSkies.travel is to bring significant organisation to the task of maintaining aviation liberalisation agreements in accordance with the intent of the signatories to such accords. Members include corporate, university and government travel managers, travel management companies and distributors, travel industry suppliers, consumer groups and travel organisations from around the world.*

SUSTAINABLE TOURISM

The Biggest but Unrecognised Challenge Facing DMO's Today

Destination Management Organisations (DMOs) have a unique historical opportunity to help lead the shift from an old and obsolete way of doing tourism to one that is regenerative rather than extractive.

By **Anna Pollock**.

After interviewing dozens of destination marketing leaders, Destination Think! identified fifty challenges facing the tourism industry. They then grouped these concerns into the following four themes: Profit and Planet; Cost and Revenue; Product and Promotion; Community and Collaboration; while also highlighting Leadership and Organization (*see Four critical trends impacting destination marketing leadership*).

What's fascinating about this list is what's absent. Virtually all the items relate to issues associated with performing a destination marketing organisation (DMO)'s traditional and primary function – i.e., doing whatever it takes to attract more visitors. The fifty concerns suggest that there is clearly an awareness of change – e.g., the shift from products to experiences; the emergence of continuously evolving, more complex and diverse media channels; the need to involve residents in tourism promotion; plus adapting to dwindling budgets, changes in consumer behaviour, tools and technology, etcetera. These are familiar, fixable problems specific to destination promotion.

By contrast, the list provides few indications that DMOs are paying much attention to the bigger, deeper, meta change drivers, the "wicked problems" and systemic risks that, according to the World Economic Forum in their Global Risk reports and the work of Goldin and Mariathasan in The Butterfly Defect, are turning the familiar upside down and will, in my opinion, necessitate a fundamental shift in DMO role and focus.

"Systemic risks are now endemic everywhere – in supply chains, pandemics, ecology and climate change, economics and politics.Failure to address these concerns will lead to greater protectionism, xenophobia, nationalism, and, inevitably deglobalization, rising inequality, conflict and slower growth…" (back cover of The Butterfly Defect).

Since all these outcomes are well known and have the potential to seriously impede tourism's progress, their exclusion from the DMO's list of concerns should be another reason for concern.

Our industry, and especially the DMOs accountable to destinations, will increasingly find itself caught between a rock and hard place. In global terms, growth would appear assured – this already huge sector has barely scratched the surface of global demand emanating from an expanding middle class in emerging markets and the global rise of Millennials and Gen Z who view international travel as both a right and rite of passage. But that same growth is clashing with the reality of expanding physical footfall on a finite, "full" planet.

Even the enlightened few who choose to go to less congested, remote places offering ever more ecological diversity and cause for wonder will, as their discoveries are shared and copied by the many, cause more harm than intended unless there are fundamental changes to business practice. The days when so-called mindful or conscious travellers could persuade themselves that their ventures into the unfamiliar are less harmful compared to those made by tourists sipping martinis by the pool in an all inclusive resort or from the top tier of a 9,000 passenger cruise liner are over. *We're ALL responsible now.* Tourism is, to use an old promotional slogan, "everybody's business" and all of us will be affected by it.

So for me, the biggest and unrecognised challenge facing tourism right now is the lack of appropriate leadership.

Old models of command and control exercised by those few that have (albeit limited) concentrations of power and budget seem bent on sustaining "business as usual" while adding comforting terms like "green" and "sustainable" to give the impression of progress.

The focus must now shift from incremental improvement to systemic transformation undertaken by everybody if we are to have any hope of staving off or minimising the aforementioned systemic risks. As long ago as 2000, W. Edward Deming, the father of Total Quality Management observed: *"Long-term commitment to new learning and new philosophy is required of any management that seeks transformation."*

A host of highly regarded thought leaders argue that transformation will require new forms of distributed, courageous, emergent, awakened, or systems leadership that is starting to emerge from the grassroots. The proliferation of awards ceremonies for innovation, imagination and effective responsibility is proof that many individual entrepreneurs are indeed already waking up, growing up and showing up.

Given the place-based nature of tourism and its utter dependence on community support for the activities of its host enterprises, DMOs have a unique historical opportunity to help lead the shift from an old and obsolete way of doing tourism to one that is regenerative rather than extractive. The first step is to acknowledge that such systemic risks are real and need to be acknowledged and addressed. But unless DMOs shift their gaze away from their growth targets and KPIs and make a commitment to "a new learning and a new philosophy" they will become increasingly irrelevant as others assume the leadership role.

Leadership, like global travel, is being democratised and nothing will be the same again.

About the author: *Anna Pollock is a vibrant thought leader, speaker, consultant and Founder of Conscious Travel, which aims to encourage healthier, more sustainable tourism business models.*

Market Intelligence Report

The information below was extracted from data available as at **06 April 2017**. By **Martin Jansen van Vuuren** of **Grant Thornton**.

ARRIVALS

The latest available data from **Statistics South Africa** is for **January 2017***:

	Current period	Change over same period last year
UK	48 165	4.1%
Germany	33 413	15.4%
USA	23 289	6.9%
India	6 293	-5.2%
China (incl Hong Kong)	12 066	28.3%
Overseas Arrivals	245 074	14%
African Arrivals	794 677	-0.3%
Total Foreign Arrivals	1 040 534	2.8%

HOTEL STATS

The latest available data from **STR Global** is for **January** to **February 2017**:

Current period	Average Room Occupancy (ARO)	Average Room Rate (ARR)	Revenue Per Available Room (RevPAR)
All Hotels in SA	63.6%	R 1 360	R 865
All 5-star hotels in SA	68.9%	R 2 565	R 1 768
All 4-star hotels in SA	65.5%	R 1 247	R 817
All 3-star hotels in SA	61.6%	R 962	R 592
Change over same period last year			
All Hotels in SA	-0.7%	7.6%	6.8%
All 5-star hotels in SA	0.3%	7.0%	7.3%
All 4-star hotels in SA	0.5%	7.4%	7.9%
All 3-star hotels in SA	0.7%	4.5%	5.2%

ACSA DATA

The latest available data from **ACSA** is for **January** to **February 2017**:

Change over same period last year	Passengers arriving on International Flights	Passengers arriving on Regional Flights	Passengers arriving on Domestic Flights
OR Tambo International	1.4%	-2.4%	-2.6%
Cape Town International	28.7%	2%	-1.7%
King Shaka International	13.4%	N/A	1.4%

CAR RENTAL DATA

The latest available data from **SAVRALA** is for **January** to **May 2016**:

	Current period	Change over same period last year
Industry Rentals	1 134 620	-1%
Industry Utilisation	74.2%	3.6%
Industry Revenue	2 375 892 450	10%

For more information contact Martin at Grant Thornton on +27 (0)21 417 8838 or visit: http://www.gt.co.za

WHAT THIS MEANS FOR MY BUSINESS

The data indicates the slowdown in domestic tourism with either low growth or a decline in passengers arriving on Domestic Flights. The decline is supported by the stagnation of occupancies of hotels. Recent political developments will lead to declining economic growth which will negatively impact on domestic tourism. The same political developments will lead to the devaluation of the Rand, which should aid foreign tourism, but these developments may also deter foreign tourists to visit South Africa despite the favourable exchange rate. **t**

*Note that African Arrivals plus Overseas Arrivals do not add to Total Foreign Arrivals due to the exclusion of unspecified arrivals, which could not be allocated to either African or Overseas.

TOURISM OUTPACING GLOBAL ECONOMY

Tourism supports 1 in 10 jobs, and is outpacing the global economy for the 6th consecutive year.

By **Annebeth Wijtenburg**.

Travel & Tourism generated 1 in 10 of the world's jobs in 2016 as the sector grew by 3.3%, outpacing the global economy for the sixth year in a row, reads a new report by the World Travel & Tourism Council (WTTC).

WTTC's Economic Impact Report 2017, which is conducted in conjunction with Oxford Economics, researches the economic impact of Travel & Tourism impact on global level, for 25 regions, and 185 countries.

According to the research, Travel & Tourism grew by 3.3% in 2016, generating US$7.6 trillion worldwide, which is 10.2% of global GDP when the direct, indirect and induced impacts are taken into account. The sector supported a total of 292 million jobs in 2016, which is 1 in 10 of all jobs in the world

Additionally, global visitor exports, which is money spent by foreign visitors, accounted for 6.6% of total world exports, and almost 30% of total world services exports.

David Scowsill, President & CEO, WTTC, said: "This is the sixth year in a row that Travel & Tourism has outpaced the global economy, showing the sector's resilience, and the eagerness of people to continue to travel and discover new places, despite economic and political challenges across the world. The continuous growth of our sector underlines the significance of business and leisure travel in driving economic development and job creation throughout the world."

Southeast Asia (8.3%) was the region with the fastest growing Travel & Tourism sector in 2016, driven by the expanding Chinese outbound market and the countries own growing markets. Latin America (0.2%) was the slowest growing region. Some countries performed well above the world average, but the Brazilian economy dragged down the whole region.

The other regions registered the following growth: South Asia (7.9%), North East Asia (4.6%), Oceania (4.4%), the Caribbean (3.2%), North America (3.1%), the Middle East (2.7%), Sub-Saharan Africa (2.4%) and Europe (1.6%).

Travel & Tourism is expected to grow by 3.8% in 2017, generating US$ 7.9 trillion. This growth is slower than previously forecast, as a result of a downgrade to the global economy and a dampening of consumer spending.

Over the next decade the sector is forecast to grow at an average of 3.9% per year. By 2027 it will generate more than 11% of the world's GDP and employ a total of 380 million people. One quarter of all jobs created in the next decade will be supported by Travel & Tourism.

Scowsill continued "The future prospects for Travel & Tourism are good, but the sector continues to face challenges. The impact of terrorism and the rise of populism pose a severe risk to the ability of people to travel efficiently and securely.

The sector itself needs urgently to address the impact of growth on destinations and its own contribution to climate change if it is to be sustainable in the long term.

The UN's 2017 International Year of Sustainable Tourism for Development is a perfect opportunity to explore solutions together.

We look forward to welcoming delegates at our upcoming WTTC Global Summit in Bangkok, Thailand, 26-27 April where these challenges will be addressed." t

About the author: Annebeth Wijtenburg is the Communications Manager at World Travel & Tourism Council (WTTC). *www.wttc.org*

WORLD TRAVEL & TOURISM COUNCIL

EXPLORING
the Wild Nature & Rich Culture of
RÉUNION ISLAND

Seemingly hidden within the currents of the Indian Ocean is a little tropical gem which calls to the heart of every traveller looking for the ultimate experience. With far reaching mountainous landscapes and strikingly beautiful terrains, **Réunion Island** holds captive a pristine historical charm, luring those looking for the perfect island getaway.

Réunion Island offers a unique blend of a tropical paradise and an adventurer's dream. With three Grande Randonnée footpaths crossing the island, you can effortlessly immerse yourself within the depths of Réunion Island's natural majesty.

The Island offers a surreal experience, as the natural lush green landscapes give way to volcanic fields of the Piton de la Fournaise. These heated volcanic fields have shaped the Island. Yet, even this momentous giant effortlessly subsides at the Island's Southern edge to a refreshing oceanic breeze.

Cast in the shadows of two prominent volcanic peaks and cliff-rimmed cirques, rests the tranquil beaches which epitomises the splendour of Reunion Island.

Réunion Island boasts not only an adventurous retreat but also a pristine natural habitat for a variety of aquatic species. The Natural Marine Reserve extends over an astounding 40 km of coastline which stretched from Cap La Houssaye in Saint-Paul to la Roche aux Oiseaux in Etang-Salé. It is within this protected Marine Reserve that the 20 km coral reef has flourished to become a unique feature encountered by visitors of Réunion Island.

With such a diverse and ecological landscape the notion of diversity appears to have been embedded within the heart of Réunion Island and its residents. Many of the inhabitants of Réunion Island are from France, Mozambique, India, China, Madagascar, the Comores and Africa, thus leading to a mixing-pot of cultural lineage that maps out the unique traditions found on Réunion Island.

Prominent influences from such a diverse heritage can be found rooted within the music and dances encountered during your stay on the Island. Maloya is a local dance and music which descends from a narrative between African and Indian music, mixed with the haunting melodies of the slaves from Africa and Madagascar.

With such diversity present on the Island and its spectacular mix of people you will find that the cuisine as well as traditions often differ. Thus, throughout your stay on the Island you can expect influences from across the globe, harnessed and captured in the delicacies offered on the Island.

It's hard to resist the beauty this island has to offer, mixed with the many aromas from the mouth-watering traditional dishes and playful dancing performed by the locals.

Image credit: Frog974 Photographies

Image: Studio Lumiere

Image: Studio Lumiere

Image credit: Lionel Ghighi

REUNION ISLAND

THE ULTIMATE EXPERIENCE

Réunion Island Tourism Board is represented by
Atout France in South Africa.

CONTACTS:

📞 **+27 010 205 0201**

✉️ **reunionisland.za@atout-france.fr**

f **GotoReunionSA**

🐦 **@reuniontourisme**

📷 **@reuniontourisme**

🏠 **blog.welcometoreunionisland.com**

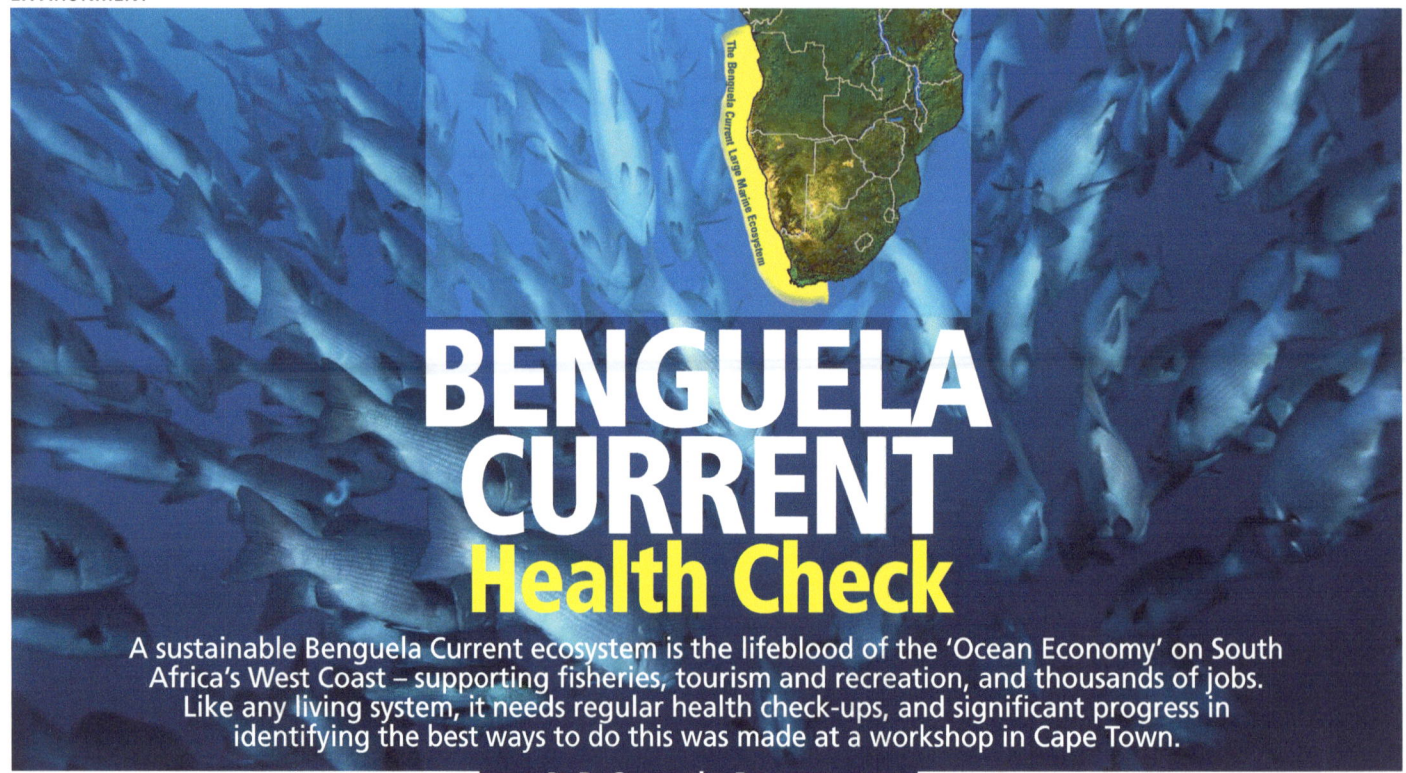

BENGUELA CURRENT
Health Check

A sustainable Benguela Current ecosystem is the lifeblood of the 'Ocean Economy' on South Africa's West Coast – supporting fisheries, tourism and recreation, and thousands of jobs. Like any living system, it needs regular health check-ups, and significant progress in identifying the best ways to do this was made at a workshop in Cape Town.

By **Dr Samantha Petersen**.

The Cape Town workshop on 23-24 March 2017 formed part of a project by the Benguela Current Convention (BCC) to strengthen the ability of member states – Namibia, Angola and South Africa – to monitor the health of the Benguela Current ecosystem in their own countries, as well as implementing an integrated approach to sustainable ecosystem management across national boundaries.

Scientists, government officials, business and civil society representatives discussed how best to measure and monitor both the economic value and environmental health of the diverse and inter-linked 'ecosystem services' provided by the ocean and coastal environment. The workshop also aimed to identify gaps in current monitoring activities and data, capacity and resource needs, and how to resolve potential conflicting uses in future.

This is vital to maintaining the sustainability of the economic and social benefits to the people who rely on the ecosystem. For South Africa, this is particularly important, given the focus on developing the maritime economy through Operation Phakisa, which has earmarked a number of diverse projects for the West Coast.

The real success of the workshops was that we achieved widespread representation from government and NGOs in sectors including mining, petroleum, environmental management, fisheries and aquaculture. From the level of engagement and participation and the positive attitude of the stakeholders, it was clear that all want to work together to achieve the same thing – to optimise the value of oceans to society over the long-term.

This bodes well for the kind of cooperation and collaboration that will be needed to manage the diverse resources and services of the Benguela Current at an ecosystem level, across traditional sector boundaries and government department 'silos'.

The productive waters of the Benguela Current support the largest portion of South Africa's commercial fisheries, and is an important area for small-scale fishing and aquaculture. The West Coast is also a hub of offshore oil and gas exploration, a focus area for the redevelopment of small harbours and coastal tourism, and home to the Saldanha Bay Industrial Development Zone. It also has a number of significant conservation areas and is attracting increasing tourism and recreation activities.

A healthy marine ecosystem provides services that have a measurable social and economic value to human well-being. Some have a direct commercial value such as fisheries, mineral and energy resources, and tourism assets, while others such as climate regulation, recreational benefits and symbolic cultural or spiritual uses, are more difficult to measure the value of.

Key recommendations from the workshops in both South Africa and Namibia included the need for a clear mechanism to perform ecosystem-based management in an integrated way across areas such as environmental management, regulation of mining and oil and gas exploration, fisheries, tourism and so on, as well as across country borders.

Participants also identified the need for working groups that incorporated the diverse sectors in order to support the integrated approach to ecosystem management, as well as the need for a central information system to serve the various sectors.

The final workshop will be held in Angola in April. Feedback from the workshops in the three countries, together with the project team's reports on linkages between ecosystem services and their value, will contribute to developing systems for integrated monitoring of the Benguela ecosystem's health and the BCC's planning for future collaborative projects and support to member states.

The Benguela Current sweeps up the South African West coast, along the entire Namibian coastline and into Angola. This creates a Large Marine Ecosystem (LME) with productive resources shared by the three countries.

The Benguela Current Convention signed by the three countries created the first LME in the world to embrace an 'ecosystem approach to ocean governance', which means managing trans-boundary resources at the ecosystem level, rather than each country acting alone and balancing human needs with conservation imperatives.

The coastal and ocean resources of the Benguela Current Large Marine Ecosystem are estimated to contribute about US$269-billion annually to the economies of Namibia, Angola and South Africa. 🆃

About the Author: Dr Samantha Petersen is the Project Leader at the Benguela Current Commission. www.benguelacc.org

Tourism Trade to Converge at
THE
HOTEL SHOW
AFRICA

Africa's biggest food and hospitality platform is set to capitalise on the booming hotel and tourism sector with buyers from across the continent and suppliers from around the world attending the event.

Leading hospitality suppliers from around the world will be in Johannesburg for the inaugural The Hotel Show Africa, which will take place from June 25 to 27.

The Hotel Show Africa 2017 will be co-located with the continent's long-established food and beverage show Africa's Big 7, making this the biggest food and hospitality platform ever, both part of Retail & Hospitality Week at The Gallagher Conference Centre.

"The Hotel Show Africa brings a new focus to the hospitality industry," says Tshifhiwa Tshivhengwa, CEO of the Federated Hospitality Association of Southern Africa (FEDHASA), which is a strategic partner for The Hotel Show.

The new event is adapted for the African market and based on international organiser dmg events MEA's highly successful The Hotel Show Dubai.

Tshivhengwa said: "A forum such as this brings a wealth of opportunity for owners, managers and suppliers in terms of connecting with each other, meeting new contacts, generating business but also for gaining essential insight and knowledge share, and FEDHASA is pleased to be a part of it."

The hospitality sector is a key growth target for governments across sub-Saharan Africa and the continent has almost 30,000 new rooms under construction at 159 hotels this year.

Top national and international suppliers have signed up to showcase hospitality products for restaurants, cafes, bars and hotels, right through to food & beverage service outlets.

Tshifhiwa Tshivhengwa, FEDHASA CEO.

Christine Davidson, Vice President, dmg events.

These include:

• Build and security, three of the world leaders: Access Control Technologies, Dormakaba and Assa Abloy.

• In the bedroom, top US mattress supplier Restonic will be at the show alongside Belgotex, which is Africa's leading flooring company, established on four continents.

• Blind Rage, promises the biggest selection of window dressings in the country, while leading furniture manufacturer Calgan Recliners will also be at the show.

• Origin Fitness brings the world's top gym equipment.

The Vision Conference runs for the full three days of the show with a strong line up of key industry speakers.

Christine Davidson, Vice President of organiser dmg events says: "We are very excited to bring a globally recognised brand to the Africa hospitality market and have been working closely with the industry to ensure the show meets the needs of all hospitality professionals. Most importantly this event focusses on how to improve guest experiences, enable closer customer engagement and increase bookings and revenue.

"So whether you own, run or operate a small, medium or large hotel, restaurant, café etc, you will come away from the event with tangible ideas, expert advice and inspiration that will ultimately help you grow your business."

The Hotel Show 2017 is part of Retail & Hospitality Week 2017 at The Gallagher Convention Centre, Johannesburg, South Africa, from June 25 to 27.

For more information visit www.thehotelshowafrica.com

The WORST HOTEL in the World

Last month I wrote about the BEST hotel I've ever stayed at, which came down to 'how did the hotel make me feel?' and led to the importance of hotel entertainment. This got me thinking of the contrary. What is the WORST hotel I have ever stayed at?

By **Guy Stehlik**.

Travelling and being in the hotel industry conjures up all sorts of both good and bad hotel memories, but I have to say, after careful thought and application of my measuring tool – how did the hotel make me feel? – I must admit to generalisation and claim that my worst hotel in the world is, in fact, a particular hotel category.

5-star hotels. There, I said it.

Dissecting my decision reveals one clear reason for my bias: expectations. I guess if you are paying in excess of R3000 per night to stay in a 5-star hotel, you have incredibly high expectations, and this is exacerbated if you are an hotelier staying in a 5-star hotel. There are very few 5-star hotels that have ever met my expectations. I can honestly say that the only 5-star hotel that has left me feeling as if this may be the 'best hotel in the world' would be a resort, or perhaps, a particular V&A Waterfront 5-star hotel.

If we look at 'value for money' (my measuring stick), in my experience, most 5-star hotels fall far short. We expect so much and we receive so little. It's not easy to put a finger on the exact problem – perhaps it stems from "hands-off" management, as in my view, most 5-star general managers are possibly the least hands-on managers in all the hotel categories. Perhaps they are too busy looking after Beyoncé or sipping Viognier with Meryl, but by no means are they concerned about any ordinary Joe, invisible even though he has paid the same rate.

And if this Joe digs deeper, the 5-star concept continues to feel like daytime robbery. Breakfast is served for a whopping R275; R40 for a local beer that's half that price at the restaurant next door; and meagre bar snacks which don't compensate. R250 for overnight parking, where the same parking bay at a 3-star hotel might be free, is crazy. Dragging your own bag through the glitzy 5-star reception, getting the up and down from the Armani-suited Food and Beverage Manager, and then schlepping your way to your room through a labyrinth of corridors, unaccompanied and unattended, armed with a faulty key card is – you guessed it – uncool!

These are some of my personal experiences that have left me with my mouth agape, wondering what my 3000 bucks were for. The answer must be 'snob value' – I guess it's so I can tell my friends I stayed here, or I can leave my key card intentionally visible at the business lunch… but deep down, I know…I'm getting taken to the cleaners. It's almost a 5-star disease.

Our local 5-star bracket needs a little introspection. I have been fortunate to experience true 5-star or even 6-star hospitality abroad, particularly in The Emirates, where staff are extremely well trained, remembering your name or your preferred drink; guests are properly profiled (there are hotels that place a photograph of your loved ones on your bedside table!); the bar snacks are unbelievable, and during dinner service the chef delights in sending through amuse-bouche. The result: guests leave feeling privileged to have experienced 'first-rate service' rather than being irked by that 'ripped off' feeling!

What is more poignant as an hotelier is the realisation that these 5-star touches haven't truly cost much at all. But they reach far into the hearts of guests.

Amuse-bouche for thought.

About the author: Guy Stehlik is the CEO and founder of BON Hotels. With an innate enthusiasm and dedication to the hotel industry, Guy's innovative and creative approach has ensured a successful and impressive career spanning many years as an hotelier and hotel owner.

For more info visit www.bonhotels.com/blog

TOURISM EDUCATION

The Move to Online Staff Training

Using online learning tools removes boardroom barriers and allows staff to learn at their own pace. So why aren't more companies – and individuals – taking their training into the digital space?

By **Nawal du Toit**.

Corporate training, as many people think, generally involves sitting in a boardroom or conference center, taking notes on branded notepads. The course or workshop might include interesting talks, team-building exercises and stacks of printed notes that may or may not be read again outside of the "classroom". Almost certainly, there will be tea and biscuits, and the time lost for training will somehow have to be made up.

There are many studies that suggest that no two people learn effectively in exactly the same way. When confronted by lengthy speeches in a classroom-like space, some may struggle to grasp the content while others will simply listen and absorb every word. Likewise, with digital learning, some may be quite happy studying in a busy, noisy office. Others, however, may prefer to learn in a quiet space in their own home.

So why aren't more companies – and individuals – taking their training into the digital space?

Using online learning tools removes barriers and allows staff the freedom to learn at their own pace – which is essential in today's fast-paced world. Staff can learn on the bus or train, in-between business commitments, while waiting for a meeting to start, or whenever else is most convenient for them.

If you're an employer setting up training for your staff, online training provides the option to simply block off time in your staff schedule that works around everything else on the agenda, instead of the other way around. There is no longer a need to sacrifice days of work to achieve the best for, and from, your employees.

With training no longer requiring individuals and teams to leave the workplace, the capacity for training in every aspect of the business can be amplified, resulting in increased productivity from the newly-upskilled team or individual.

There are many online courses that are suited to the travel, tourism and hospitality industry – from basic service and/or management skills to personal selling skills that could boost an employee's career.

In South Africa, Educate24 offers short courses, developed by top academics, on Customer Relationship Management, Developing People, Hotel Housekeeping, Working in a Hotel, Restaurant Service Basics, and Customer Service Skills, to name a few. There are over 75 very affordable courses available to teach the core skills that employees need for staff to excel at their jobs.

Additionally, by taking your staff training online, employers will be able to track the progress of each individual. This will give your human resource department a clear indication of which employees have an aptitude for a specific field and which employees require more development. In essence, employers will have a birds eye view of where the strengths lie within their workforce, and be able to utilise that to maximum effect.

Everyone, from chief executives to maintenance staff, deserve access to quality training that will allow them to fulfil their potential.

About the Author: Nawal du Toit is the General Manager of digital training platform Educate24. www.educate24.co.za

```
Q L B T I V B E J N C J P F Z X H R P I O Z R O O Z J I U H T L T V E B Q
P U S U R T Q W J L T M U Q A M I W R W K L C S B Z F Y X L E F A Z X V R
I X L W B S H C J D G T B J H X K E I Y Q J Z T G R O O X K V L T T X Q U
G R K R H R P U J O B I E X V H S D E S C F Q S C D F W Q U T X L D F N
L E B A K N S Q C D V M I F A P F R V T V S K F K T J X Y Z O J S Q R D
S S Q I M E P C L R J E Z B O P R R A J V U T Q G G I X Q Q L W Y I O O Q
B J S Q I H X H G Z A Y S T B W U Z L M U Z M D B D P W A E D W W E G O V
O S J M Q P I Z G Z H L S U R S F X B S A G L J Z Y H P R F Z H D O A N A
W Q S L D C X S E K O I S H I E M T W Q L R J D A D M A M H L H V H X O S
M C P U U H P E W A R A C V Z J T K C A G D C K B T T G C A S W C F Z S A
L E Q W B Y B K H H H Z U Q Y J S E A V D O A I B O X M I U H N N S R E P
L Q F A S T J C J M I M Q A Q R G C N T C W Y T K T E A F S A Q J F R B
A H J L D Z A M H R T P C J Q R A W Y S T P O I H L Y Z Q B Z Q I J C M I
Y K R M O K Y J X A T S K P M T B H B F L S K B S T R I V Z E U J W G Y H
Z A X I T N T R O W A R S C L X Z E H R G N Q H A T Q S D Z G C A E E L T
I N G V W Y I K X N F J J H W Y A B Q T N L L D S Y L D V A P E N W C A K
V F Z D E E N F Z P T G C K E P M G X P Y K F M X F V T A Y M V D M Z I H
Q T S G U M J C E C H F A Z E D N W G A B G P S F N A Q X Y E N S X U M D
D N L A M W L G O W C M X R P L F J X S I W X E P P K M V D R Z R C A D Y
R R I V G Z F E N I L X I V W X Q J I P M S F S D Z Y Z D Q C U H L Q N K
H O K Z A A A T G O G R V W C A K Q W C Z Y F Z P U V Y G W K N L U N L V
N A G N O B P E T X Z S Q L O M X I N H S J N B L P T A C H E B Q V F B Q
H P W D E W N B O G L I K K V Q M Q Z P B D Y N Y C F D Z D J G T G K X C
U G F Q M N C Q K P Z G Q G E W R C G L H K L X L O K L J C W E J C V V P
J S A V S J J Z D F Q J Z T D C G H H J S Q Y F T I I V F L J N V C N Q U
O M Y T A F G V V L H K W N H N Q O J V Z Z V L D L T E B V G W J S V D S
K I I G S X Y O Q V Q O T P A X U Z A A K Y M S H R V T P A N B B D K K J
B I X X H P L B N H P R M G X D J A I V E C I J Y F Y E F V J Z V C B T A
T O M B K B I Q K J L M O Z O N U R S V P H V J Z X X R H S L N E X H T Y
V G B B T N M X N J A B C P C O S W J O B R P D H I E O X U Y P K X L R Z
V W J R E A E S C C E P M C P E K U K Q T O M D R U E T H J S M C P M X L
Q Q X G R R W Z H L S W W B V D E Z D P N W M C E W Q X C T T H P I Y G F
K P Z I W Q L W L H H X K V N K Z A L X G V L V E F Q S C P T V R D K Q A
O L A Y R A W E G M A R K A H N Q O T W Q V U V G I B S J T N G U B R T T
C M G R G O F D Y S J W R J X Z K N Q E T O U B D C C L B D Y Q W B W N H
Y H S T D J F E T F Z F J X S X W K K M X Y Z Z U Y T C A P R Z X P J S B
R U R D F R Z B F S W S L L E W D Q Y M C Y F G Z R J G Q Q U I L M A M R
Q L D R S P V Q Z L Q I G W P T M E X U O J M J I W J S Y S G O E I J T G
R N P Q K B C L L J A E C Z G R H Z E H Z G M I O O R X C Y T T M I L K R
E W M M D B B B V X Q W G F K E M W E R C X J Q B X P S T K G Y G S L A K
K O S C K N G E N C A K G N J J P C F C A Z V S F Z D X Y F Z J T S L E B
J N P F B Z R S O G J D Q S X A G P J Y H B L R F C H A B R P K F F Q H E
C L Z E F F L P U S H M K R J E I G A R S G E J E Z F K T U E W F D A L J
D K A X T F Q T D R Y L W C Y L B G F W V C S U J B V T P F U S P V P I B
O T W S P I T G W M S U G Z M P M Z R O H I Y Q G K F C V J T K C P D S X
```

THERE ARE TWENTY NAMES IN THIS WORDSEARCH, BUT YOU ONLY SAW ONE. WEAR A LIFEJACKET.

VOLUNTEERLAND

Findings from the latest WYSE Travel Confederation report on volunteer travel, suggest that voluntourism contributes towards the UN Sustainable Development Goals, brings tourism spend into local economies, and fosters a form of cultural exchange deemed mutually beneficial by all stakeholders.

By **Jennifer Woodbridge**.

Economists estimate that at least 971 million people volunteer each year across the globe, whether through an organisation or other intermediary or directly with persons outside of one's household (Salamon et al).

The sheer number of volunteers has led to a comparative reference – 'Volunteerland'. If the world's volunteers were to form a single country, known as Volunteerland, they would form the largest adult population in the world, behind only China.

Their total economic value is estimated at more than 1.3 trillion US dollars – making Volunteerland the seventh largest economy in the world, behind the US, Japan, Germany, China, the UK and France.

tourism, and fosters a form of cultural exchange deemed mutually beneficial by all stakeholders.

Projects hosting international volunteers also reported being highly satisfied with both their professional relationships with volunteer-sending organisations and preparedness levels of the volunteers those organisations send.

As volunteer travellers are hosted by a project and community, the global association representing businesses involved in youth, student and educational travel, WYSE Travel Confederation, and its Cultural Exchange Advisory Panel, endeavoured to gain a better understanding of the benefits of volunteer travel for not only travellers, but the projects and local communities hosting visiting volunteers.

However, within youth travel, WYSE Travel Confederation estimates volunteer travel as one of the smaller sectors or niches of youth travel as a whole. It accounts for about 2% to 5% of global youth travel or 5.4 to 10+ million arrivals of the 270+ million. The reason for what seems to be an imprecise range is that young travellers typically have multiple purposes for travelling and volunteer activities could be undertaken as part of a trip with other purposes, such as an academic or gap year abroad, language immersion, an internship, or even a hybrid volunteer-holiday trip.

That said, volunteer travel can be viewed as high impact when we look at the benefits for the traveller, the volunteer project, and the local host community.

Findings outlined in the latest WYSE Travel Confederation report on volunteer travel, 'Project perspectives on the benefits of volunteer travel' suggest that international volunteering contributes towards the UN Sustainable Development Goals, brings tourism spend into local economies that might not otherwise benefit from mainstream

"When you consider the benefits for the traveller, the volunteer project, and the local host community, volunteer travel is high impact," said David Chapman, Director General of WYSE Travel Confederation.

Volunteer travel is popular among young people who would like a unique experience combining work and travel. It accounts for an estimated 2 to 5 percent of global youth travel or 5.4 to 10 million of the more than 270 million arrivals per year. Volunteers contribute a considerable number of work days and spend in local economies and, according to WYSE Travel Confederation research, are among those young travellers that stay the longest and spend the most.

"Negative media attention on international volunteering has portrayed the volunteer travel experience as the province of the privileged simply wanting to broaden their cultural knowledge at the expense of others. This is not an accurate or fair picture," said Bastian Weinberger, a member of the WYSE Travel Confederation Cultural Exchange Advisory Panel and Chief Executive Officer of Smaller Earth, a UK-based company specialised in work experience travel for young people.

VOLUNTEER PROJECTS AND THE UN SUSTAINABLE DEVELOPMENT GOALS

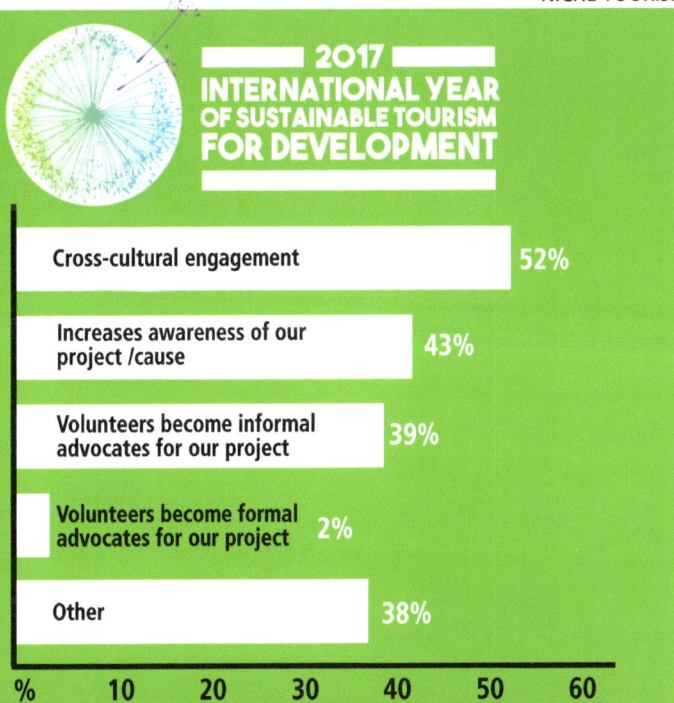

2017 INTERNATIONAL YEAR OF SUSTAINABLE TOURISM FOR DEVELOPMENT

The projects surveyed in the WYSE Travel Confederation report on volunteer travel were asked about the contribution of volunteers to the UN's Sustainable Development Goals (SDGs). The SDGs that the projects think are the most supported by volunteers were inclusive and equitable education and ensuring healthy lives. The support for educational goals is logical in terms of the large number of educational projects covered by the survey.

Other goals mentioned by the projects themselves include:

- Assisting /inspiring local teachers with new ways of teaching.
- Creating awareness around real animal numbers through accurate monitoring and identification.
- Educating the locals on animal welfare and pet care.
- Improving and promoting sustainable lifestyles.
- Mitigating human-wildlife conflicts.
- Promoting multicultural understanding and world peace.
- Providing for the wellbeing of people living with mental and physical disabilities.

Cross-cultural engagement **52%**

Increases awareness of our project /cause **43%**

Volunteers become informal advocates for our project **39%**

Volunteers become formal advocates for our project **2%**

Other **38%**

% 10 20 30 40 50 60

If the world's volunteers were to form a single country, known as Volunteerland, they would form the largest adult population in the world. Their total economic value is estimated at more than 1.3 trillion USD – making Volunteerland the seventh largest economy in the world.

"Project perspectives on the benefits of volunteer travel is specifically about the organisations and communities hosting volunteer travellers and their opinions on international volunteer experiences," explained Weinberger.

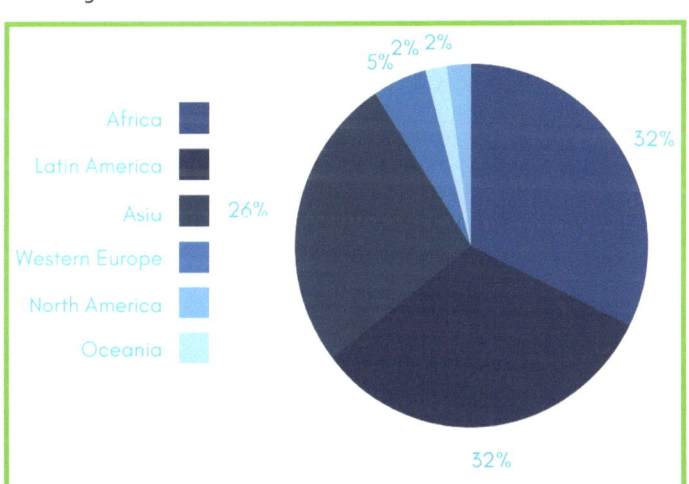

- Africa
- Latin America
- Asia — 26%
- Western Europe
- North America
- Oceania

5% 2% 2%
32%
32%

Projects by region: The distribution of volunteer projects in the report emphasises their concentration in the Global South, with Africa, Latin America and Asia accounting for over 90% of reported projects.

The unbalanced media portrayal of international volunteering was debated at last year's World Youth and Student Travel Conference (WYSTC). Part of the discussion highlighted that travellers contemplating international volunteer experiences have access to more ratings and reviews than ever before and that this has led to a 'cleaning up' of the sector. This has been viewed positively by stakeholders who adhere to best practices and quality standards. There was also consensus that a travel trade association like WYSE Travel Confederation helps to differentiate the good players from the bad ones.

Projects hosting volunteers believe that UN Sustainable Development Goals numbers 3 and 4, Good Health and Well-Being and Quality Education, were most supported by the work done by international volunteers, according to the report.

The report, Project perspectives on the benefits of volunteer travel, is the second part of a project examining the perceived benefits of international volunteer travel.

The first part of the project focussed on the opinions of young volunteer travellers and culminated in the publication Development through volunteering overseas: Perceptions on personal and project based impact. Both reports are free to download from the WYSE Travel Confederation website.

www.wysetc.org/wp-content/uploads/2017/03/Benefits-of-volunteer-travel.pdf

---

About WYSE: The World Youth, Student and Educational (WYSE) Travel Confederation is a global not-for-profit membership organisation dedicated to promoting and developing opportunities for the youth, student and educational travel industry.

WYSE Travel Confederation is committed to understanding the ever-changing characteristics, motivations and needs of young travellers. By gathering, analysing and sharing important market intelligence with members, academics and government decision-makers, the unique fast-changing needs of the youth market is at the forefront of its activities as it seeks to accelerate the development of youth travel. WYSE Travel Confederation, a long-standing Affiliate Member of UNWTO, is the world's most powerful network of youth and student travel professionals, connecting travel industry players with decision-makers and government officials.

Founded in 2006 and created from the merger of the Federation of International Youth Travel Organisations (FIYTO) and the International Student Travel Confederation (ISTC), both formed after World War II to inspire young people through international travel and to help remove cultural barriers, WYSE Travel Confederation brings together 60 years of global youth and student travel expertise.

For more information about WYSE Travel Confederation, visit www.wysetc.org

VEHICLE REVIEW

On the road with the
MAZDA3
Astina
2.0 Automatic

By **Tessa Buhrmann**.

As a motorist, there's nothing more comforting than knowing that you're safely ensconced in a car that takes passenger safety seriously. Especially when that car is as good looking as the new-look Mazda3 2.0 Astina Plus Auto! And we had the privilege of being ensconced in this beauty on a recent road-trip down the KwaZulu-Natal South Coast.

In keeping with Mazda's KODO design language, the Mazda3 Astina looks and feels beautiful. It is a hatchback with style – its coupe-like stance, sleek sporty lines and classy interior with sport-style seats, heads-up display, cruise-control and paddle-shift – all combine to ensure a great road-trip. And it has a reverse camera.

With my hubby happily taking charge of the wheel I soon had our mobile connectivity sorted and our destination entered using the MZD connectivity system with its Bluetooth, navigation system and 7" touchscreen. Mazda's SKYACTIV Technology ensured that the Astina delivered an exciting and responsive drive that was agile and handled well (and yes, I managed to wrestle my hubby out of the driver's seat a couple of times). The 2.0L engine with its 6-speed automatic gearbox certainly delivered on both performance and economy, with our road trip averaging 7.0L/100km.

But for me, it was the super-cool 'intelligent' safety features that stood out. I loved that the car has 'Smart City Brake Support' (a system to detect the risk of collisions at low speeds and great for traffic situations) and Blind Spot Monitoring – you can't but help notice the warning that flashes on the head-up display and wing mirror.

And then there's the Adaptive LED Headlights that recognise leading and oncoming cars and turn off selected LEDs to avoid blinding other drivers… and when driving at low speeds the wide-range low beam expands to increase driver visibility! The Lane Departure Warning and Lane Keep Assist alert the driver when there is an 'unintentional lane departure' – the cool thing is that when accompanied by acceleration or turn signal operation it recognises the move as intentional.

One really useful safety feature when on a long road-trip is the Driver Attention Alert which is designed to reduce accidents caused by 'inattentiveness due to driver fatigue'. The system, which is activated at speeds above 65 km/h, begins to "learn" the driver's habits, watching inputs and the vehicle's movements in the early stages of a journey. Later, if the system detects changes in vehicle behaviour suggesting that the driver may be losing concentration, it will advise a rest stop by sounding a chime and displaying a warning in the information system. Like I said, one seriously intelligent car!

We certainly found the Mazda3 Astina a fun car to drive and in addition to being really good to look at, it is pretty robust too – surviving one of the South Coast's infamous potholes really well, with not even a flat tyre. 🄣

About the author: Tourism Tattler correspondent **Tessa Buhrmann** is the editor of **Responsible Traveller** magazine. *www.responsibletraveller.co.za*

FAST FACTS: Mazda3 2.0 Astina Plus Auto

Price:	R415,900 (Incl VAT)
Engine:	2.0-litre 4-cylinder petrol
Compression ratio:	14.0 : 1
Maximum power:	121kW @ 6000rpm
Maximum torque:	210Nm @ 4000rpm
Fuel consumption:	5.9 l/100km (combined)
Warranty:	3-year unlimited kilometer factory warranty factory warranty
	3-year roadside assistance
	3-year service plan
	5-year Corrosion Warranty.